SCHOLASTIC

Read & Practice Mini-Books

GRAMMAR & PUNCTUATION

10 Interactive Mini-Books That Help Students Build
Grammar & Punctuation Skills—Independently!

BY KAREN KELLAHER

NEW YORK • TORONTO • LONDON • AUCKLAND • SYDNEY
MEXICO CITY • NEW DELHI • HONG KONG • BUENOS AIRES

Teaching *Resources*

For Anna with love.

Edited and produced by Immacula A. Rhodes
Cover design by Jason Robinson
Interior illustrations by Mike Moran
Interior design by Kathy Massaro

ISBN-13: 978-0-439-45341-7
ISBN-10: 0-439-45341-0

Contents

Read & Practice Mini-Books: About the Series

I f you're like many teachers, you may have trouble mustering enthusiasm and confidence when it's time to teach about subject-predicate agreement, tricky homophones, or plural possessives. One reason is that many of today's educators grew up during the 1970s and '80s, when schools began backing away from the direct instruction of standard English conventions. At the time, many educators felt that grammar, spelling, and punctuation could be adequately addressed during the editing process.

It didn't always work. Nearly two decades later, college professors noted that an alarming number of incoming students could not properly punctuate a paragraph or distinguish between an adjective and adverb. Universities began pushing for more direct and rigorous teaching of English fundamentals.

Today, your mandate as a language-arts teacher is clear. According to national and state standards, our second-, third-, and fourth-graders must demonstrate a sound understanding of sentence structure, grammar, punctuation, capitalization, and spelling. They must also apply this understanding to their own writing.

This return to grammar and spelling need not mean boring worksheets, however. In *Read & Practice Mini-Books: Grammar & Punctuation*, we offer exciting activities that will motivate your class to become better readers and writers. Your students will have a blast assembling the books, reading them together, and tackling the interactive practice pages that address subjects and predicates, run-ons, capitalization, commas, question marks, quotation marks, and more. The *Read & Practice Mini-Books* series includes three additional books: *Vocabulary*, *Parts of Speech*, and *Spelling*.

How to Assemble the Mini-Books

Teacher Preparation:

1. Carefully remove the perforated pages from the book.

2. Make double-sided copies of the mini-book pages on standard $8\frac{1}{2}$- by 11-inch paper.

Student Assembly:

3. Fold each page in half along the solid line.

4. Place the pages in numerical order and staple along the spine.

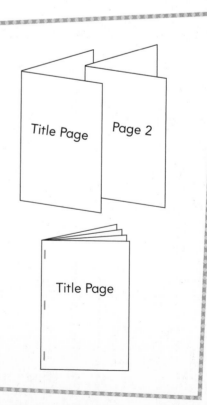

The Sentence Recipe

Subjects and Predicates

Name _____

☆ **Show What You Know!** ☆

Make sentences by combining each **complete subject** in Box A with a **complete predicate** in Box B. Write your sentences next to the correct numbers below.

Box A

1. The fire fighter
2. My teacher
3. The lion
4. The rain
5. Sarah's computer

Box B

roared loudly.
broke yesterday.
wrote on the board.
carried a hose.
fell from the sky.

1. _____

2. _____

3. _____

4. _____

5. _____

Go Further: Write your own sentence. Circle the complete subject. Underline the complete predicate.

11

Once upon a time, in Grammar City, two chefs heard about an exciting contest. A prize was being offered to the person who could cook up the most interesting and delightful sentence.

Now, neither chef had much experience in this area. But each one was sure that he or she could whip up a spectacular sentence. And so the contest began.

1

---

2 A sentence must also have a PREDICATE.

The predicate is the part of the sentence that tells what the subject did or what happened to the subject.

There are two ways of looking at the predicate. The **simple** predicate is the verb of the sentence. The **complete** predicate is the verb plus any words that describe it.

✳ **Simple Predicate:**

Two cuddly kittens <u>played</u> happily.

✳ **Complete Predicate:**

Two cuddly kittens <u>played happily.</u>

☆ ☆ **Sentence Secret** ☆ ☆
☆ ☆

If a sentence is missing a subject or a predicate, it is called a fragment!

10

Read & Practice Mini-Books: Grammar & Punctuation © 2009 Karen Kellaher, Scholastic Teaching Resources

The first chef, named Sue, went to work right away. She put a big mixing bowl on her counter and began gathering her favorite words.

It just so happened that Sue was particularly fond of subjects. She loved words that named people, places, and things. And so that is what Sue placed in her bowl first. She tossed in her favorite noun:

KITTENS

2

Sentence Recipe

Follow the prize-winning recipe for a good sentence!

1 A sentence must have a SUBJECT.

The subject can be a **noun** (a person, place or thing). Or it can be a **pronoun** (like *I, you, he, she, it, we,* or *they*). The subject tells who or what the sentence is about.

There are two ways of looking at the subject. The **simple** subject is the noun or pronoun by itself. The **complete** subject is the noun or pronoun along with any words that describe it.

 Simple Subject:
Two cuddly <u>kittens</u> played happily.

 Complete Subject:
<u>Two cuddly kittens</u> played happily.

9

Read a Puzzle Mini-Book: Grammar & Punctuation © 2009 Karen Kellaher, Scholastic Teaching Resources

Sue peered inside her bowl. The word KITTENS looked lonely in there by itself. So Sue decided to add some other words.

First she tossed in the adjective TWO. "That's a little better," thought Sue. "But my recipe still needs something."

Sue thought for a moment. Then she added the word CUDDLY to her recipe. She studied her work:

TWO CUDDLY KITTENS

Sue smiled. She was sure that she would win the sentence contest.

3

Each chef thought about what the other had said. Then, suddenly, both of them got the same idea.

"Why don't we . . ." started Sue.

". . . put our two recipes together?" finished Pete. And that is exactly what they did. The two chefs combined their ingredients to make the super sentence."

TWO CUDDLY KITTENS PLAYED HAPPILY.

They blended Sue's interesting subject with Pete's action-packed predicate. And they won the top prize in the sentence recipe contest!

8

Across town, another chef was busy in his kitchen. His name was Pete. Like Sue, Pete wanted to win the prize. And like Sue, he believed he could cook up a perfect sentence.

Pete searched his cabinets for the finest ingredients. Soon he spotted the perfect verb:

PLAYED

4

Sue revealed her secret recipe first. She showed Pete her collection of words:

TWO CUDDLY KITTENS

"Interesting. But where is the action?" Pete said. "What did these two cuddly kittens do? You need a verb."

Next, Pete showed Sue his sentence recipe:

PLAYED HAPPILY

Sue frowned. "Your recipe is full of action," she said. "But who or what did the action? You need a subject, or your recipe will never win."

7

Pete was very happy. He liked action words, and he especially liked the verb PLAYED. But he wasn't sure if one word would be enough to please the judges. So Pete added the word HAPPILY to his sentence recipe. Now his creation read:

PLAYED HAPPILY

"It's perfect!" Pete exclaimed. "That prize is mine!"

5

On the day of the contest, both chefs raced to the spot where the recipes would be judged. They were surprised to see a long line of other chefs already waiting there.

Sue and Pete stood beside one another in line. After a while, they began to chat. They agreed to show one another their sentences.

6

Read & Practice Mini-Books: Grammar & Punctuation © 2009 Karen Kellaher, Scholastic Teaching Resources

Stop That Sentence!

Identifying Run-Ons

Name _____

☆ ☆ ☆ ☆
☆ ## Show What You Know! ☆ ☆
☆

Put an *R* in front of each run-on. Put an *S* in front of each correct sentence.

____ 1. Mom said we can ride bikes after school she said we must do our homework first.

____ 2. The basketball team won the first game.

____ 3. My glass is full of orange juice.

____ 4. My kite is broken will you help me fix it?

____ 5. Tracey has that book at home.

____ 6. The dog wagged his tail he wanted a treat.

____ 7. I have taken piano lessons for three years I have learned a lot.

____ 8. The mail carrier delivered a package.

Go Further: On a separate sheet of paper, fix each run-on above. You can break the run-on into two smaller sentences. You can also sometimes add joining words like "and" or "but" to turn a run-on into a correct sentence. Here's an example:

Fran likes lemons, but she hates limes.

11

Stop That Sentence!

One day in Grammar City, Gary the Grammar Cop was having a cup of coffee at the station when he received an urgent call.

"Gary, we have a problem," the caller said. "Sentences are out of control all over the city. They just run on and on and don't make any sense. You must do something!"

1

How do you think Gary the Grammar Cop fixed the run-on in the menu? Show how you would fix the run-on sentence on the lines below. Don't forget to use a capital letter at the start of each sentence and punctuation at the end of each sentence.

10

Gary the Grammar Cop was getting tired and hungry. He had caught a lot of rule-breakers! Gary decided to stop for some lunch at the diner.

When Gary opened the menu, he groaned. A run-on was on the first page! It said:

> **Our cheeseburger is served with salad and French fries we also have hot soup today for $1.95.**

Gary fixed the run-on and ordered a cheeseburger—without soup. It looked like it was going to be a long day!

9

Gary put down his cup and hurried for the door. He knew that run-on sentences could spell trouble.

As he set out for downtown, Gary knew what to look for—sentences that go on for far too long and express more than one idea without correct punctuation. He had seen these rule-breakers before.

2

Gary decided to stop at the grocery store first. Just as he suspected, he spotted a run-on right on the window of the store! A bright yellow sign read:

Green beans are on sale for just 85 cents a pound fresh peaches are now in stock.

Gary knew that the best way to stop a run-on was to break it into two or more smaller sentences. And that's what he did.

3

How do you think Gary the Grammar Cop should fix the run-on at the school? Show how you would fix the run-on sentence on the lines below. Don't forget to use a capital letter at the start of each sentence and punctuation at the end of each sentence.

8

How do you think Gary the Grammar Cop should fix the run-on at the grocery store? Show how you would fix the run-on sentence on the lines below. Don't forget to use a capital letter at the start of each sentence and punctuation at the end of each sentence.

_____

_____

_____

_____

_____

_____

4

Gary kept looking for run-ons. As he drove, he saw another one on the sign in front of the school. The big sign said:

> **School will be closed next week for spring break enjoy your time off.**

Gary shook his head. A school was not a good place for rule-breaking run-ons. But he knew he could solve the problem quickly.

7

With that problem solved, Gary got back in his car and searched for other rule-breaking run-ons. It did not take long. Soon, Gary spotted a run-on at the shoe store. A note was taped to the door of the store. It said:

I left to have lunch at the deli I will be back in one hour thank you very much.

"This is a bad one," Gary thought to himself. "I must deal with this run-on very carefully."

5

How do you think Gary the Grammar Cop should fix the run-on at the shoe store? Show how you would fix the run-on sentence on the lines below. Don't forget to use a capital letter at the start of each sentence and punctuation at the end of each sentence.

_____

_____

_____

_____

_____

_____

6

Uppercase Idol!

Capitalization

Name _____

15

☆ Show What You Know! ☆

Underline the word in each sentence that should be capitalized.

1. Tim just read a spiderman comic book.

2. My dad said i can go to the party.

3. We have one week off in march.

4. let's do a jigsaw puzzle after school.

5. We live in arizona, where it is hot and dry.

6. I told jennifer she could borrow the book.

7. The space telescope took photos of mars.

8. Our gym teacher is Mr. newman.

Go Further: Find three words that are capitalized in a magazine, newspaper, book, menu, or other everyday item. For each word, write a sentence to explain why that word needs to be capitalized.

Get ready, judges! It's time for the Uppercase Idol Contest!

In each round of this contest, you will read a sentence. There are three underlined words in each sentence. Only one underlined word deserves to be capitalized. Which one is it? You be the judge! Choose the word that you think needs a capital letter. Then turn the page to see if you are correct—and why!

Judges, let's review! We gave capital letters to:

❋ **The pronoun I**

❋ **The first word in a sentence**

❋ **Names of specific people**

❋ **Names of specific places**

❋ **Names of specific things**

When you are writing, remember to capitalize these very important words!

And that concludes our Uppercase Idol Contest!

Now, it's time for Round 1 of Uppercase Idol. Let's begin!

Sentence 1

Today, i will bake cookies with my cousin.

Which underlined word needs a capital letter? Why?

2

The correct answers are... *Ann, Florida,* and *December.* These three words are all proper nouns. *Ann* names a specific person, *Florida* names a specific place, and *December* names a specific thing.

Ann
Florida
December

13

The correct answer is . . . the word *I*. The word *I* is a pronoun that you use when you are talking about yourself. Whenever you write this pronoun, you must use a capital letter. Do you need help remembering this rule? Just tell yourself that *I* am important, so *I* need a capital letter.

This is how Sentence 1 should look:

Today, I will bake cookies with my cousin.

3

Nice work, judges! Now, it's time for our surprise Bonus Round! In this round, you'll be given a sentence. You must decide which three words in that sentence need a capital letter. Ready? Here's the sentence:

Bonus Round

Our teacher asked ann to tell about the trip she took to florida in december.

Which three words need a capital letter? Why?

12

The correct answer is. . .the word *Saturday.*

It is a proper noun, just like *Kyle* and *Boston.*

It names a specific thing. *Saturday* names a specific day of the week.

Here are some other proper nouns that name specific things. They all need capital letters:

Nintendo *(names a specific brand of toy)*

April *(names a specific month)*

Thanksgiving *(names a specific holiday)*

The Little Mermaid *(names a specific book)*

This is how Sentence 5 should look:

We have our first soccer game at 9:30 on Saturday.

11

Let's move on to Round 2 in the Uppercase Idol Contest! See what you think!

Sentence 2

the roses are finally in <u>bloom.</u>

Which underlined word needs a capital letter? Why?

4

The answer is . . . the word *The*. This word may seem like a tiny, unimportant word. But it needs a capital letter because it is at the beginning of the sentence. The first word in a sentence always gets capitalized. It tells readers that a new sentence is starting!

This is how Sentence 2 should look:

☆
☆
☆
The roses are finally in bloom. ☆
☆
☆

5

Let's go to Round 5 of the Uppercase Idol Contest! Judges, check out this sentence!

☆
☆
☆
| **Sentence 5** | ☆ |
☆
☆

We have our first soccer game at 9:30 on saturday.

Which underlined word needs a capital letter? Why?

10

Great job so far, judges! Now try Round 3.

Sentence 3

Please tell <u>kyle</u> to <u>go</u> back to his seat <u>now</u>.

Which underlined word needs a capital letter? Why?

6

The answer is... the word *Boston*. Boston is the name of a specific place. It is a proper noun.

Other place names that should be capitalized are specific states, countries, continents, and even streets and stores. Here are some examples:

Texas   **ShopRite**

Australia   **Elm Street**

North America   **Oakwood School**

This is how Sentence 4 should look:

I am going to Boston next week if the weather stays nice.

9

The right answer is . . . the word *Kyle*. This word needs to be capitalized because it is the name of a person. It is an example of a proper noun.

Proper nouns are names of **specific** people, places, and things. They always begin with capital letters. Look at these examples:

✻ **The teacher wrote on the board.**

(The word teacher does not need a capital because it does not name a specific person.)

✻ **Mrs. Johnson wrote on the board.**

(Mrs. Johnson needs to be capitalized because it names a specific person.)

This is how Sentence 3 should look:

☆
☆
☆

Please tell Kyle to go back to his seat now.

☆
☆
☆

⬡ 7

Are you ready for Round 4? Here it is!

☆
☆
☆

Sentence 4

☆
☆
☆

I am going to <u>boston</u> next <u>week</u> if the <u>weather</u> stays nice.

Which underlined word needs a capital letter? Why?

⬡ 8

The Sentence Enders

Sentence-Ending Punctuation

Name _____

☆ Show What You Know! ☆

Circle the correct ending punctuation for each sentence.

1. Lily has blonde hair   .   ?   !

2. Where is the remote control   .   ?   !

3. This is an emergency   .   ?   !

4. Do you have a pet   .   ?   !

5. Go inside for lunch now   .   ?   !

6. We have a spelling test today   .   ?   !

7. Asia is a continent   .   ?   !

8. Please pass the salt   .   ?   !

Go Further: Look for an example of each kind of sentence in a magazine or newspaper. Share your examples with the class.

11

Did you know that there are different kinds of sentences? Each one has its own punctuation mark. Read this funny story to learn what makes each kind of sentence special—and what kind of punctuation to use at the end!

1

☆ ☆ ☆ **Write like Ivan!** ☆ ☆ ☆

An **imperative** sentence is one that gives a command, or order. An imperative sentence may end in a period or an exclamation point.

Write your own imperative sentence here:

_____

_____

_____

When you write, remember the story of the four brothers. Know what kind of sentence you are writing. Don't forget to use a period, question mark, or exclamation point!

10

The Sentence Enders

Once, there were four brothers. Their names were Declarative Dave, Interrogative Terry, Exclamatory Ed, and Imperative Ivan. From the time they were small, the boys had very different personalities.

Come down the hall.

The youngest brother, Imperative Ivan, was quite bossy. He told everyone in the family what to do. Sometimes he remembered his manners. Sometimes he did not. Ivan would demand:

Please get me a cookie.

Give me that ball!

Take me to the playground.

Come down the hall.

Usually Ivan used a period to end his sentences. But sometimes, if he was feeling especially bossy, he used an exclamation point.

2

9

Declarative Dave thought he knew everything. And he was not afraid to show it. Dave was always sharing facts with the rest of the family. Dave would say:

Texas is the biggest state.

A koala is not a bear.

Our house is painted yellow.

A female horse is called a mare.

Our house is painted yellow.

When Dave wrote his facts down, he ended each one with a period.

3

☆ ☆ ☆ **Write like Ed!** ☆ ☆ ☆

An **exclamatory** sentence is one that expresses strong feelings, like fear, happiness, or anger. An exclamatory sentence ends in an exclamation point.

Write your own exclamatory sentence here:

_____

_____

_____

_____

8

☆ ☆ ☆ **Write like Dave!** ☆ ☆
☆ ☆

A **declarative** sentence is one that states a fact. A declarative sentence ends in a period.

Write your own declarative sentence here:

_____

_____

_____

_____

_____

_____

4

The third brother, Exclamatory Ed, was very anxious and excited. Ed did not speak much. But when he did, everyone listened. That's because Ed usually had important news to report. Ed would exclaim:

There's a fire in the kitchen!

Help! I hurt my face!

I am so proud of you!

Hurray! We won the race!

When Ed wrote his sentences down, he ended each one with an exclamation point.

7

Interrogative Terry was not as sure of himself. In fact, Terry was not sure of anything at all. He was always asking questions. Terry would ask:

Who was George Washington?

Why is the sky blue?

When is the first day of spring?

Where is my other shoe?

Where is my other shoe?

When Terry wrote his questions down, he ended each one with a question mark.

5

☆ ☆ ☆ **Write like Terry!** ☆ ☆ ☆

An **interrogative** sentence is one that asks a question. It starts with *who, what, when, where, why, how, is, are, do, can,* or other question words. An interrogative sentence ends in a question mark.

Write your own interrogative sentence here:

6

Comma Connie

A Story About Using Commas

Name _____

☆ Show What You Know! ☆

There is at least one comma missing from each sentence. Add commas where they are needed.

1. Oliver lives in Miami Florida.

2. Mary was born on January 12 2001.

3. Seattle Washington is a rainy city.

4. I would like puzzles games and books for my birthday.

5. We saw a gorilla tiger panda and kangaroo at the zoo on Tuesday.

6. "Please set the table" said Mom.

7. July 4 1776 was an important date in history.

8. Mr. Bryant shouted "Watch out!"

Go Further: Commas can also be used to separate clauses in a sentence. Here is one example:

We heard a noise, which turned out to be thunder.

Write another example here, or find one in a newspaper or magazine:

_____

_____

_____

11

There once was an old woman named Comma Connie. She was always poking her nose into other people's business. Comma Connie did not want to miss out on anything! Everywhere Connie went, she left commas behind.

When Comma Connie saw someone was making a list for the grocery store, she just had to take a look.

Store List
We need
bread, milk,
eggs, apples,
and shampoo.

Can you find some clues that Comma Connie was looking at this list? Circle them!

As Comma Connie shows, you should use a comma to separate a direct quote from the rest of the sentence. A direct quote is someone's exact words. Here are two examples:

"I like oatmeal," said Jack.

Pam said, "I prefer pancakes."

Write your own direct quote here. Use a comma to separate it from the rest of the sentence.

_____

_____

_____

Store List
We need
bread, milk,
eggs, apples,
and shampoo.

As Comma Connie shows, you should use commas to separate items in a list.

Write your own sentence that has a list of items:

Use commas to separate the items:

_____

_____

_____

2

Of course, Comma Connie's favorite thing to do was to read the newspaper. That's where she learned what was going on around town. One day, Connie read:

★ NEWS

New Park Will Open Downtown

A new park will open next year. It will be on Spring Street. "It will be a great place for children to play," says the mayor.

Can you find a clue that Comma Connie was reading this newspaper article? Circle it!

9

One time, Comma Connie noticed that a neighbor was writing invitations to a party. Connie read the invitations. She wanted to know the date of the party.

Can you find the clue that Comma Connie was looking at the invitation? Circle it!

As Comma Connie shows, you should use commas when you write a letter. Use a comma to separate your opening from the body of the letter. Use another comma between your closing and your name.

Write an example of an opening or closing of a letter. Remember to use a comma:

_____

_____

As Comma Connie shows, you should use a comma when you write the date. A comma separates the month and day from the year.

Write today's date here. Use a comma between the day and year:

_____

4

Comma Connie was getting nosier and nosier. One day, she saw a friend writing a letter. Connie wondered whom the letter was for. So she looked over her friend's shoulder.

Dear Dad,
Happy birthday.
I hope you
have a great
day. Love,
Your Daughter

Can you find two clues that Comma Connie was reading this letter? Circle them!

7

Another day, Comma Connie heard her friends talking about taking a trip. Connie just had to know where they were going, so she took a peek at their calendar.

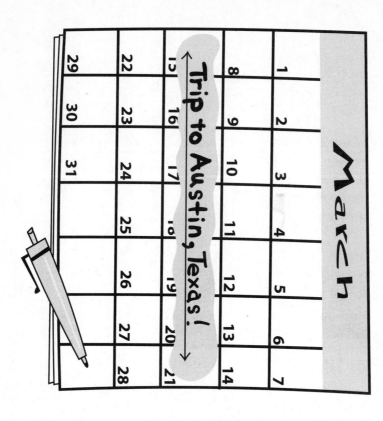

March

1	2	3	4	5	6	7
8	9	10	11	12	13	14
15	16	17	18	19	20	21
22	23	24	25	26	27	28
29	30	31				

Trip to Austin, Texas!

Can you find the clue that Comma Connie was looking at the calendar? Circle it!

Welcome Austin, Texas

As Comma Connie shows, you should use a comma to separate the name of a city or town from the state.

Write your own town and state here. Use a comma to separate the two words:

_____

_____

☆ ☆ ☆
☆ **Show What You Know!** ☆ ☆
☆

Add quotation marks to each sentence.

1. Push me higher! the child shouted.

2. My mom said, Don't forget your lunch.

3. My birthday is coming up, Victoria said.

4. I yelled, Here I come!

5. Who knows the answer? the teacher asked.

6. The cookie is delicious, I said.

7. My brother exclaimed, It's my turn!

8. Good morning, said the waitress.

Go Further: Ask a friend what he or she would do as class president. Write your friend's exact words as a quotation. Remember to follow the rules from the mini-book.

11

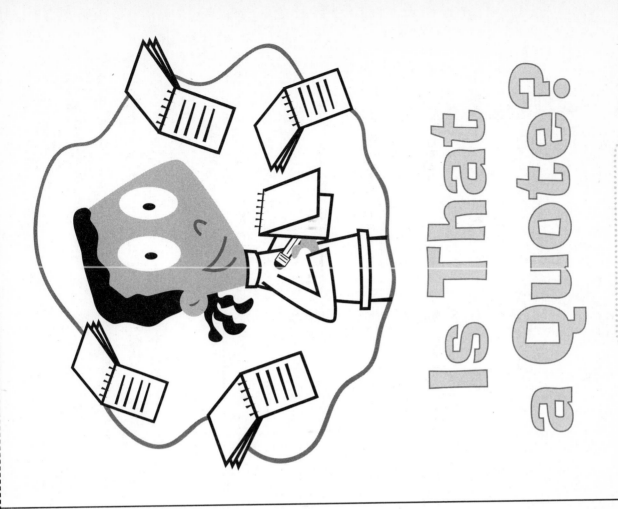

Is That a Quote?

Quotation Marks

Name _____

Hi there! My name is Robin. My class is getting ready to vote for class president. I am writing a story about the election for our class newspaper. Join me as I talk to the five students who want to be president!

First, I talk to Justin. I ask Justin why he wants to be the class president. Justin says that he wants to change the school lunches. He says that our lunches should be healthier and tastier.

"It is time for a change in the cafeteria!" Justin says.

I write this down.

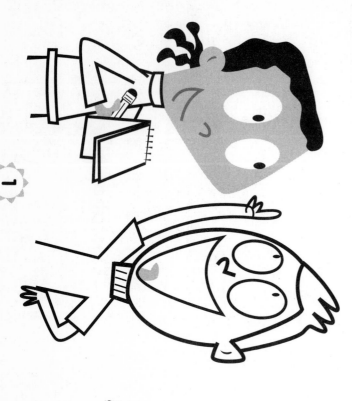

"I think our class is ready for some fun projects!" Kelsey says.

Do you see how I punctuated Kelsey's words? The exclamation point is inside the quotation marks. When you write a quote, put the punctuation that goes with what the person says **inside** the quotation marks.

Finally, I talk with Kelsey. She tells me why she would make a good president. She says that she has some exciting ideas for our class. One idea is a big recycling project. Another idea is a class play.

"I think our class is ready for some fun projects!" Kelsey says.

I write this down.

9

Did you notice how I used quotation marks to show Justin's **exact** words? You can only use quotation marks when you know exactly what a person said.

2

Next, I talk to Kate. Kate tells me that if she is picked as class president, she will try to make recess longer. Our recess is 15 minutes long. Kate thinks it should be 20 minutes long.

"Kids need more time to have fun," Kate says.

I write this down.

Do you notice something different? This time I put the words *He says* and a comma **before** the quote. This is another way to show who is talking.

Do you see how I used quotation marks at the **beginning** and **ending** of Kate's words? It is important to remember both spots!

Next, I spot Lamont. He wants to be class president, too. I ask him why. Lamont smiles. He tells me that he thinks our class gets too much homework. If he gets to be president, he will ask the teacher for less homework.

He says, "Homework is no fun!"
I write this down.

I see Liam next. I tell him about my newspaper story. Liam explains that he wants more class parties. That is why he wants to be president. We already have parties for Thanksgiving and Valentine's Day. Liam thinks we should have parties for Flag Day and Earth Day, too.

"I promise more cupcakes and cookies!" Liam says.

I write this down.

5

"I promise more cupcakes and cookies!" Liam says.

Do you notice that I put the words *Liam says* **after** the quote? This is one way to show who is talking. You can also use other words. For example:

Liam shouts
Liam explains
Liam mutters

6

Apostrophe on the Move

Apostrophes in Contractions

Name _____

☆ **Show What You Know!** ☆

It's your turn to make letters disappear! Read each word pair. Then remove letters and add an apostrophe to make a contraction. Write your contraction on the line.

1. could not _____

2. she is _____

3. it is _____

4. they will _____

5. are not _____

6. we are _____

Go Further: This sign was on the library wall:

> Please don't make loud noises or you'll be asked to leave.

How many letters did Apostrophe eat? _____

Rewrite the sign the way it looked before Apostrophe came along!

_____

_____

11

Once upon a time, there was a tiny elf named Apostrophe. Apostrophe had a very strange habit. He liked to eat letters! Apostrophe ate all kinds. Apostrophe stole letters from signs, menus, newspapers, and books. Each time, he left behind a tiny curved fingerprint that looked like this: '

1

We will have storytime at 2:00.

The librarian appeared from behind a giant stack of books.

"May I help you?" she asked Apostrophe. When Apostrophe explained that he was looking for a job, the librarian smiled. "You're hired!" she exclaimed. "I have too much work to do by myself."

And that is how Apostrophe found himself in a new town, with a new home and a new job where he could munch to his heart's content. He knew that it would be a very long time before he ran out of letters again.

10

Everyone in the village had heard of Apostrophe. They got used to finding letters missing from their signs and books. They would wake up to find that:

❋ *Can not* had become *can't.*

❋ *I am* had become *I'm.*

The villagers did not mind so much. But after a while, Apostrophe began to run out of letters to eat. It was time to move to a new town.

2

Soon, the doctor came out to talk to Apostrophe. He explained that he did not need any more workers in his office. But he told Apostrophe to try the library.

Apostrophe walked down the street to the town library. As he entered the door, his eyes opened wide. The library was full of signs, posters, newspapers, magazines, and books, books, books! It was a feast!

9

• Apostrophe on the Move • Read & Practice Mini-Books: Grammar & Punctuation © 2009 Karen Kellaher, Scholastic Teaching Resources

Apostrophe packed his things and caught a bus to a new town. The journey seemed to take forever. During the trip, Apostrophe's stomach began to growl. He was hungry. Apostrophe swiped an o from a sign on the bus window.

3

Apostrophe sat and waited. But soon, he got hungry again. His mouth watered as he looked at the sign on the desk. He told himself that it could not hurt to have a light snack. So he took the letters w and i from the doctor's sign. Now the sign said:

Have a seat. We'll be right with you.

8

At the beginning of the bus trip, the sign had said:

Please do not stand while the bus is moving.

At the end of the trip, the sign said:

Please don't stand while the bus is moving.

No one seemed to notice. Apostrophe got off at the next stop.

4

Next, Apostrophe decided to get a job.

First, he tried to find work in a doctor's office.

When he walked up to the desk, he saw a sign.

It said:

Have a seat. We will be right with you.

7

The new town seemed pleasant. Apostrophe knew that the first thing he should do was to find a place to live. He saw a big sign in front of an apartment building. It said:

Rooms for Rent!
They are large and have great views.

5

Apostrophe could not resist. On his way past, he grabbed an *a* from the sign. Now it said:

Rooms for Rent!
They're large and have great views.

Apostrophe knocked on the door of the building. When a woman answered, he explained that he was looking for a place to live. The kind woman was happy to rent him a room.

6

Apostrophe Strikes Again!

Apostrophes in Possessives

Name _____

7

☆ ☆ ☆ **Show What You Know!** ☆ ☆ ☆

Add an apostrophe (') or **'s** to make each underlined noun a possessive. Write the possessive on the line.

1. The car that belongs to <u>Frank</u> is _____ car.

2. The collar that belongs to the <u>dog</u> is the _____ collar.

3. The engine on the <u>train</u> is the _____ engine.

4. The tail of the <u>fish</u> is the _____ tail.

5. The toys that belong to the <u>kids</u> are the _____ toys.

6. The coats that belong to the <u>Gunnings</u> are the _____ coats.

7. The restroom for <u>men</u> is the _____ restroom.

8. The eyes of the <u>deer</u> are the _____ eyes.

Go Further: Find an apostrophe in a magazine, book, or newspaper. Tell whether it is used to show possession or to make a contraction of two words.

Apostrophe was a tiny elf who liked to munch on letters. When he took a letter, he always left behind a tiny curved fingerprint.

✳ **We *will*** became **we'll** when Apostrophe ate the *w* and *i*.

✳ ***I am*** became ***I'm*** when Apostrophe ate the *a*.

Apostrophe was a nice guy, and sometimes he felt sorry for stealing letters. He decided to find a way to make it up to the people of his town.

Apostrophe knew that he could not stop eating letters. They were just too good. But he had an idea. He could bring gifts to the townspeople!

1

✳ In Apostrophe's notes, he uses apostrophes to show possession, or ownership. For example:

Mary's clock is the clock that belongs to Mary.
Dan's dog is the dog that belongs to Dan.

✳ How do you make a singular noun possessive? Apostrophe tells us to add 's. For example:

The library's books
Chris's flowers

✳ How do you make a plural noun possessive? If the plural noun ends in s, Apostrophe tells us to add an apostrophe after the **s**. For example:

The Smiths' picture

✳ Of course, there are some plural nouns that do not end in s. These nouns need an 's to become possessive. For example:

The children's cupcakes
The geese's beaks
The women's suitcases

6

Apostrophe's last gift was for the children of the town. Once, Apostrophe had nibbled on the sign in front of the school. Apostrophe wanted the children to know that he was sorry. He baked a special treat for the children and left it in the school office. He put a note on the box that said:

The children's cupcakes.

Finally, Apostrophe smiled. He had given everyone something special.

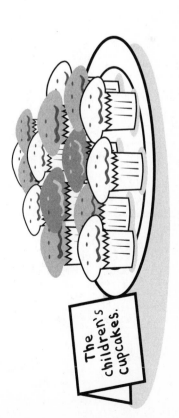

Can you find Apostrophe's fingerprint on the note?

5

First, Apostrophe collected a big bag of new books for the library. It was full of picture books, dictionaries, mysteries, and more. Apostrophe left the gift by the front door of the library. On the bag, he put a note. It said:

The library's books.

Apostrophe had not eaten any letters from the note. But he had touched the note. He had still left his tiny curved fingerprint behind.

Can you find Apostrophe's fingerprint on the note?

2

Next, Apostrophe wanted to say thank-you to Chris, the nice woman who owned the building where he lived. Chris loved flowers, so Apostrophe bought some pretty tulips and roses. He brought the flowers home to Chris, along with a nice note that said:

Chris's flowers.

Can you find Apostrophe's fingerprint on the note?

3

Mr. and Mrs. Smith were next on Apostrophe's list. The Smiths owned the grocery store in the town. Apostrophe was always swiping letters from their signs. To show that he was thankful, Apostrophe drew a picture for Mr. and Mrs. Smith. He sent it to the grocery store with a note that said:

The Smiths' picture.

Can you find Apostrophe's fingerprint on the note?

4

☆ ☆ Show What You Know! ☆ ☆

Write the correct abbreviation for each underlined word or phrase.

1. I live at 44 North Ridge Avenue. _____

2. Mister Nelson gave out the pencils. _____

3. Piper's birthday is October 7. _____

4. Let's meet at the park on Saturday! _____

5. We live in the United States. _____

6. His name is Zachary Bohm, Junior. _____

7. My friend works for Scholastic, Incorporated. _____

8. Mail this to Oak Street School. _____

Go Further: Write your own address, including your street, city, and state. What abbreviations can you use?

11

For Short

Abbreviations

Name _____

Shorty B. McShort was always in a hurry. He was a busy man with places to go and people to see. To save time, Shorty used shortcuts when he wrote. These shortcuts are called abbreviations and acronyms. They are shortened forms of everyday words.

One day at work, Shorty got a terrible headache. The headache got worse and worse. Shorty called his doctor to make an appointment. Then he wrote his boss a note. It said:

Dear Mr. Wright,
I must leave work 15 minutes early today. I am going to see Dr. Jones.

Circle the abbreviations that Shorty used in his note. Do you know what they stand for? Turn the page upside down to find out!

Mr. = Mister; Dr. = Doctor

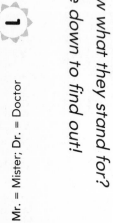

The next day, Shorty made an amazing discovery. His headache was gone! It looked like slowing down and having fun was a good idea after all!

When Shorty got to the doctor's office, he had to fill out some paperwork. The papers asked for his name and address. Shorty wrote:

Shorty McShort
33 Speedy St.
Apt. 2-A
Philadelphia, Pa.

Circle the abbreviations that Shorty used. Do you know what they stand for? Turn the page upside down to find out!

2

St. = Street; Apt. = Apartment;
Pa. = Pennsylvania

Shorty's dad did not listen to him. He came by to pick Shorty up for the game anyway. And Shorty was surprised to find that he had a great time! He did not worry about what time it was or what he had to do next. Best of all, his favorite team won the game! At the end of the game the scoreboard read:

Home   67 pts.
Visitor 63 pts.

Circle the abbreviation that Shorty saw on the scoreboard. Do you know what it stands for? Turn the page upside down to find out!

6

pts. = points

Dr. Jones examined Shorty. But she could not figure out the reason for his headache. She told Shorty to get some rest and relaxation. Then she told Shorty to come back for another appointment in two weeks.

On his way out, Shorty made his appointment. He wrote the date and time on a little card. It said:

Remember doctor check-up
Fri., Jan. 15
11:00 a.m.

Circle the abbreviations that Shorty used.
Do you know what they stand for?
Turn the page upside down to find out!

3

Fri. = Friday; Jan. = January, a.m. = ante meridiem (that's Latin for "before noon" or morning)

Shorty's dad e-mailed him back. He asked why Shorty could not go. Shorty explained:

I have to finish a report for work. It is due A.S.A.P. I am only on p. 40!

Circle the abbreviations that Shorty used.
Do you know what they stand for?
Turn the page upside down to find out!

8

A.S.A.P. = as soon as possible; p. = page

Shorty set out for home. On his way, he stopped at a store for some groceries. He pulled his shopping list from his pocket to see what he needed. The list said:

One qt. milk
One lb. grapes
One doz. eggs

Circle the abbreviations that Shorty used.
Do you know what they stand for?
Turn the page upside down to find out!

4

qt. = quart; lb. = pound
(from the Latin word "libra,"
meaning pound); doz. = dozen

After his very salty supper, Shorty checked his e-mail. There was a message from his dad. It said:

I have two tickets for the basketball
game tonight!
I will pick you up at 7 p.m.

Shorty had no time for a basketball game. He e-mailed his dad back:

Sorry, Dad.
I'm too busy.
Maybe we can
go in Feb.
Love, Shorty

Circle the abbreviations that Shorty and his
dad used. Do you know what they stand for?
Turn the page upside down to find out!

7

p.m. = post meridiem
(Latin for "after noon");
Feb. = February

Shorty waited in line for five whole minutes to pay for his groceries. He tapped his fingers on the counter. He checked his watch and saw that it was getting late.

On his way home, Shorty drove as fast as he could. He made sure to check the speed limit first. The sign said:

> **Speed limit**
> **45 m.p.h.**

Circle the abbreviation that Shorty saw.
Do you know what it stands for?
Turn the page upside down to find out!

5

m.p.h. = miles per hour

At home, Shorty tried to cook dinner. But it was a disaster! That's because Shorty was in too much of a hurry. He did not read the recipe very carefully. The recipe said:

> **Add 1 tsp. salt**

But poor Shorty thought the recipe said:

> **Add 1 c. of salt**

It was a small mistake, but it made a big difference!

Circle the abbreviations on this page.
Do you know what they stand for?
Turn the page upside down to find out!

6

tsp. = teaspoon; c. = cup

☆ ☆ Show What You Know! ☆ ☆ ☆

Find the punctuation marks in the sentences. Write the letter for each mark next to the sentence that uses it.

A. underline   D. colon
B. parentheses   E. ellipses
C. hyphen   F. semicolon

_____ 1. The children said, "I pledge allegiance to… the United States of America."

_____ 2. I just read Charlotte's Web.

_____ 3. There are seventeen kids in the class; nine of them are girls.

_____ 4. Erik has three dogs: Jasper, Vic, and Bud.

_____ 5. My new shirt is red (my favorite color).

_____ 6. We had old-fashioned sundaes.

Go Further: Write your own sentence using one of these unusual forms of punctuation. Share it with the class.

7

Punctuation Trading Cards

includes 1 stick of gum

Punctuation Pro • Collection •

Six Unusual Punctuation Marks

Name _____

Name: Colon

Appearance: Two periods, one above the other.

Where Found: The colon is usually spotted introducing lists or separating the hour from the minutes when telling time.

Examples: I want three things for my birthday: a kazoo, a magic set, and a bike.

We begin school at 8:35 a.m.

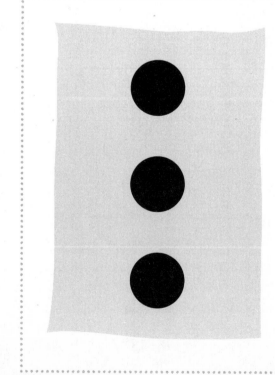

1

Name: Ellipses

Appearance: Three periods in a row.

Where Found: Ellipses often signal that words have been left out of a sentence on purpose.

Examples: The children sang the song together: "The wheels on the bus go 'round and 'round...all through the town."

6

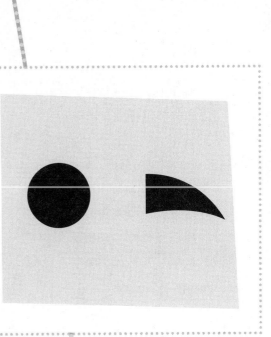

Name: Semicolon

Appearance: A period above a comma.

Where Found: The semicolon is usually found joining two related sentences together to make one sentence.

Examples: Please leave the window open; we like the fresh air.

Pete said he would be at the party; his sister Gabby cannot come.

2

Underline

Name: Underline

Appearance: A line under a piece of writing.

Where Found: An underline is often spotted under the title of a book, newspaper, movie, or TV show.

Examples: Kelly's favorite book is <u>Amber Brown Is Not a Crayon.</u>

5

Punctuation Pro Collection • Read & Practice Mini-Books: Grammar & Punctuation © 2009 Karen Kellaher, Scholastic Teaching Resources

3

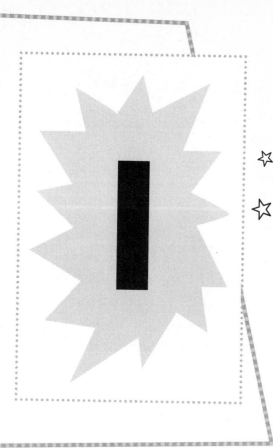

Name: Hyphen

Appearance: A short dash.

Where Found: The hyphen is often seen connecting two-part words. It also divides a word that must be separated at the end of a line of writing.

Examples: The blue-eyed girl smiled.

Everyone in the class agrees that choco-late is a delicious food.

4

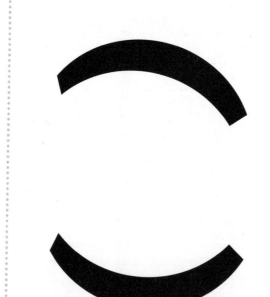

Name: Parentheses

Appearance: Looks like two curved edges of a circle. Parentheses are always seen in pairs.

Where Found: Parentheses hold extra information.

Examples: We will go away during spring break (April 9 to 16).

 # Answers

The Sentence Recipe

page 11: 1. The firefighter carried a hose.
2. My teacher wrote on the board. 3. The lion roared loudly. 4. The rain fell from the sky.
5. Sarah's computer broke yesterday.
GO FURTHER: Responses will vary.

Stop That Sentence!

page 4: Green beans are on sale for just 85 cents a pound. Fresh peaches are now in stock.

page 6: I left to have lunch at the deli. I will be back in one hour. Thank you very much.

page 8: School will be closed next week for spring break. Enjoy your time off.

page 10: Our cheeseburger is served with salad and French fries. We also have hot soup today for $1.95.

page 11: 1. R, 2. S, 3. S, 4. R, 5. S, 6. R, 7. R, 8. S
GO FURTHER: 1. Mom said we can ride bikes after school. She said we must do our homework first. 4. My kite is broken. Will you help me fix it? 6. The dog wagged his tail. He wanted a treat. 7. I have taken piano lessons for three years. I have learned a lot.

Uppercase Idol

page 15: 1. Spiderman, 2. I, 3. March, 4. Let's, 5. Arizona, 6. Jennifer, 7. Mars, 8. Newman
GO FURTHER: Responses will vary.

The Sentence Enders

pages 4, 6, 8, and 10: Answers will vary.

page 11: 1. period, 2. question mark, 3. exclamation point, 4. question mark, 5. period, 6. period, 7. period, 8. period
GO FURTHER: Responses will vary.

Read & Practice Mini-Books: Grammar & Punctuation
© 2009 by Karen Kellaher, Scholastic Teaching Resources

Comma Connie

pages 2, 4, 6, 8, and 10: Answers will vary.

page 11: 1. Oliver lives in Miami, Florida. 2. Mary was born on January 12, 2001. 3. Seattle, Washington is a rainy city. 4. I would like puzzles, games, and books for my birthday. 5. We saw a gorilla, tiger, panda, and kangaroo at the zoo on Tuesday. 6. "Please set the table," said Mom. 7. July 4, 1776 was an important date in history. 8. Mr. Bryant shouted, "Watch out!"

Go Further: Answers will vary.

Is That a Quote?

page 11: 1. "Push me higher!" the child shouted. 2. My mom said, "Don't forget your lunch." 3. "My birthday is coming up," Victoria said. 4. I yelled, "Here I come!" 5. "Who knows the answer?" the teacher asked. 6. "The cookie is delicious," I said. 7. My brother exclaimed, "It's my turn!" 8. "Good morning," said the waitress.

Go Further: Responses will vary.

Apostrophe on the Move

page 11: 1. couldn't, 2. she's, 3. it's, 4. they'll, 5. aren't, 6. we're

Go Further: Apostrophe ate 3 letters. The sign read: Please do not make loud noises or you will be asked to leave.

Apostrophe Strikes Again!

Apostrophe left his fingerprint in: library's (page 2), Chris's (page 3), Smiths' (page 4), children's (page 5)

page 11: 1. Frank's, 2. dog's, 3. train's, 4. fish's, 5. kids', 6. Gunnings', 7. men's, 8. deer's

Go Further: Responses will vary.

For Short

page 11: 1. Ave., 2. Mr., 3. Oct., 4. Sat., 5. U.S., 6. Jr., 7. Inc., 8. St.

Go Further: Responses will vary.

Punctuation Pro Collection

page 7: 1. E, 2. A, 3. F, 4. D, 5. B, 6. C

Go Further: Responses will vary.

Read & Practice Mini-Books: Grammar & Punctuation
© 2009 by Karen Kellaher, Scholastic Teaching Resources